Playground Games and How To Play Them

by Jenny Alexander

Contents

Section 1
1	Ball Games	2
2	Skipping Games	6

Section 2
3	Hiding and Seeking	12
4	Hiding and Sneaking	14

Section 3
5	Dips and Tags	18
6	More Catching Games	20

Index of Games — 24

Edinburgh Gate
Harlow, Essex

1 BALL GAMES

Ball Statues

Number of players: 5+

How to play

1. Stand in a big circle.

2. Throw the ball to each other. You can throw it to any player you like.

3. If you drop the ball, freeze like a statue. Stay frozen while the others keep playing.

4. The winner is the last one left when everyone else has turned into a statue.

You will need

a ball and a big space

You will need
a ball

Piggy in the Middle

Number of players: 3+

How to play

1. Decide who is going to be the piggy. The piggy stands in the middle.

2. The other two players throw the ball to each other over the piggy's head. The piggy tries to catch it.

3. If the piggy catches the ball, the player who threw it swaps places with the piggy.

4. If a lot of people want to play you can have two or three piggies in the middle.

> **You will need**
>
> a ball and a wall

Matthew, Mark, Luke and John

Number of players: 2+

How to play

1. Stand in a line facing the wall.
2. Throw the ball against the wall and catch it as you say this rhyme:

   *Matthew, Mark, Luke and John
   Let your neighbour carry on …*

3. When you say "on", step away and let the next player take over. That player catches the ball and says the rhyme. When the player gets to the word "on", the next player takes over.
4. Pass the ball up and down the line in this way. If you drop it, you are out.
5. The winner is the last one left in.

2 SKIPPING GAMES

I Like Coffee, I Like Tea

Number of players: 2

How to play

1 Start off skipping on your own. As you skip, say this rhyme. Put your friend's name in it:

> *I like coffee, I like tea,*
> *I like Darren in with me!*

2 Your friend jumps in and skips with you. Now say:

> *I don't like coffee, I don't like tea,*
> *I don't like Darren in with me!*

3 Your friend jumps out again.

4 Keep going until you trip. Then swap over and start again.

You will need

a short skipping rope

You will need
a long skipping rope

Teddy Bear, Teddy Bear

Number of players: 4+

How to play

1   Pick two people to turn the rope.
2   The rest of the players stand in a line.

3   One at a time, jump in and skip to this rhyme. Do the actions as you say it.

> *Teddy bear, teddy bear*
> *Touch the ground,*
> *Teddy bear, teddy bear*
> *Turn around.*
> *Teddy bear, teddy bear*
> *Go upstairs,*
> *Teddy bear, teddy bear*
> *Say your prayers.*
> *Teddy bear, teddy bear*
> *Switch off the light,*
> *Teddy bear, teddy bear*
> *Say goodnight.*

4   If you stop the rope or miss any of the actions you are out. Swap with one of the people turning the rope.

Granny's in the Kitchen

Number of players: 4+

How to play

1. Pick two people to turn the rope.
2. The rest of the players stand in a line.
3. The first person jumps in and skips. You all say:

   *Granny's in the kitchen,
   doing a bit of stitching.
   In comes the bogeyman
   to chase granny out!*

4. Then the second person jumps in and they skip together. You all say:

   *Oh! said granny, that's not fair –
   Oh! said the bogeyman, I don't care!*

You will need

a long skipping rope

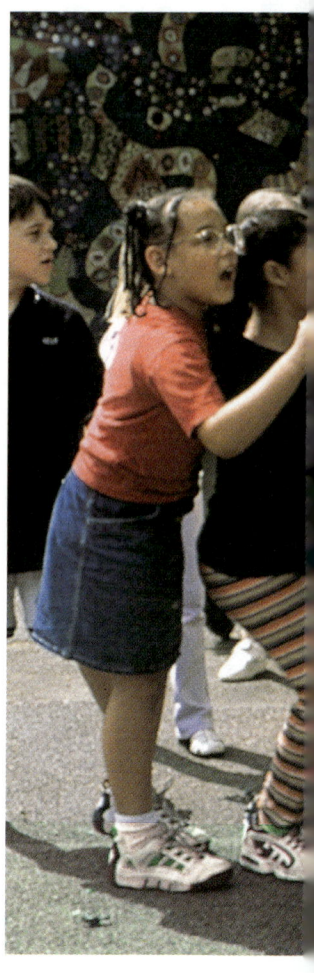

5   The first skipper goes out, and the second one becomes granny.

6   Start again.

7   If you stop the rope or jump in too slowly you are out. Swap with one of the people turning the rope.

3 HIDING AND SEEKING

Hide and Seek

Number of players: 3+

How to play

1   Choose the seeker and decide how much time everyone should have to hide. You could do it like this:

   - Make the seeker turn his back.
   - One of you run your hand over his back, saying:

     *Snakey, snakey on your back,
     Which finger did that?*

   - As you say "that", poke his back with one finger.
   - Ask him to guess which finger it was. If he guesses first time, you have five seconds to hide in. If he guesses second time, you have ten seconds. And so on.

2   The seeker covers his eyes and counts the seconds out loud. Everybody else hides.

3   When he has finished counting, the seeker shouts, "Coming – ready or not!" If he finds you, you are out.

4   The winner is the last person to be found.

You will need

nothing

You will need

nothing

40–40

Number of players: 3+

How to play

1. First choose a home base.
2. Now decide who is going to be the seeker. Do "snakey, snakey" to see how long she must give you to hide.
3. Run and hide while the seeker covers her eyes.
4. When she comes looking for you, try to slip past her to get to the home base without her seeing you.
5. If you reach it, shout "40–40 in!" But if she sees you, she shouts "40–40 out!" and says your name. Then you are out.
6. The game ends when everyone has been spotted or got home. The first one out becomes the seeker for the next game.

Note: Sometimes the seeker might want to be lazy and just hang around near the home base waiting for the others to come. This is called "egg-laying", and it isn't allowed.

4   HIDING AND SNEAKING

There are lots of games where one person hides their eyes and everyone else tries to sneak up on them. Here are two of them.

Grandmother's Footsteps

Number of players: 3+

How to play

1   First decide who is going to be Grandmother (or Grandfather). The other players line up against a wall or on a line in the playground.

2   Next, Grandmother goes about 50 paces away and turns her back on you.

3   Now try to creep up on her. Every time she turns around, freeze. If she doesn't see you move, stay where you are. If she sees you, go back to the line and start again.

4   The first player to touch Grandmother is the winner. They become Grandmother (or Grandfather) in the next game.

You will need

a wall or line

There are two other ways of playing Grandmother's Footsteps. In both of them, Grandmother keeps her back turned all the time.

Colours

Grandmother calls out a colour, and if you are wearing anything of that colour, you can take one step forward. The first person to touch her shoulder wins.

Letters

This is the same as the colours game, but Grandmother calls out a letter. Take one step forward for each time the letter appears in your name. For example, if your name is Anna Smith, take one step for *M*, but two steps for *N*.

What's the Time, Mr Wolf?

Number of players: 3+

> **You will need**
>
> a wall or line

How to play

1. First decide who is going to be Mr Wolf (or Mrs Wolf).

2. The rest of you stand on the line, while Mr Wolf takes fifty paces forward. He turns his back on you.

3. All creep a little way towards him, then stop and say, "What's the time, Mr Wolf?" If Mr Wolf says a time like "3 o'clock" or "11 o'clock", he keeps his back turned and everyone is safe.

4 Continue creeping forward a bit more. Then stop and ask him again.

5 When he thinks you are getting close, Mr Wolf will answer, "Dinner time!" Then he will turn and chase you all back to the line.

6 If he catches you, you become the wolf. If he doesn't catch anyone, he has to be the wolf again.

5 DIPS AND TAGS

In catching games someone has to be "it" and try to catch or tag the others. Use a dip to decide who is going to be "it". Try one of these.

Dips

Ip, dip, sky blue
It won't be you!

Each peach pear plum
Out goes Tom Thumb
Tom Thumb won't do
Out goes Betty Blue
Betty Blue won't go
So out goes you!

Ip, dip, dip
My little ship
Sailing on the water
Like a cup and saucer
O-U-T spells out!

Eeeny meeny
Macca racca
Rare rye
Domi nacca
Chicka racca
Chicka racca
Om pom push!

There are lots of names for catching games, including "Tag", "Tig", "It" and "He". You don't need any special equipment, just a lot of space. As few as two people can play, or as many as twenty. Here are three ways to play.

Tag

1. First decide who is "it", and everyone else run away.
2. If he tags or touches you, you are "it".
3. Try to tag someone else so that they will become "it" in your place.

Chain Tag

1. Play this like tag, but if the catcher tags you, join hands with him.
2. Now you are both "it". When you tag another player, she must join hands too.
3. But when the next person is tagged the chain splits into two twos.
4. The game ends when everyone is caught.

Hospital Tag

1. In this game, if you are tagged you don't become "it". You have to hold the part of your body where you were tagged.
2. If you get tagged again, you have to hold that part of your body with your other hand.
3. The third time you are tagged, you become "it" because you have run out of hands!

6 MORE CATCHING GAMES

Stuck in the Mud 1

Number of players: 3+

The idea of the game

When the catcher tags another player, they are stuck in the mud and can't run away any more. If the catcher can get all the players stuck in the mud, he wins.

How to play

1 The game starts like any other catching game, with the catcher trying to tag the other players.

2 If you are tagged, stand still with your arms out to show you are stuck in the mud.

3 Any player who is still free can rescue the ones who are stuck in the mud by touching them on the arm.

4 If a large number of people want to play, have more than one catcher.

Stuck in the Mud 2

How to play

1. In this version, players who are stuck in the mud stand with their arms out and their legs wide apart.

2. Players who are still free can only rescue them by crawling between their legs.

Shipwrecked

Number of players: 4+

The idea of the game

The catcher is a hungry shark. The rest of the players pretend to be shipwrecked, and the playground is the sea. There are bits of wreckage to cling to, but not enough for everyone.

How to play

1. First decide what to use for wreckage. Choose things like trees, drainpipes or shapes painted on the playground. Have one piece of wreckage less than the number of shipwrecked sailors.

2. Now run away from the shark. Grab hold of a piece of wreckage so that he or she can't get you.

3. If someone else arrives at your piece of wreckage, you have to move on because only one player is allowed on each piece of wreckage at a time.

4. If you are caught you become the shark.

5. There is always someone in the water for the shark to chase, and the game goes on until everyone is too worn out to play any more!

INDEX OF GAMES

40–40	13
Ball Statues	2
Chain Tag	19
Dips	18
Grandmother's Footsteps	14
Granny's in the Kitchen	10
Hide and Seek	12
Hospital Tag	19
I Like Coffee, I Like Tea	6
Matthew, Mark, Luke and John	5
Piggy in the Middle	4
Shipwrecked	22
Stuck in the Mud 1	20
Stuck in the Mud 2	21
Tag	19
Teddy Bear, Teddy Bear	8
What's the Time, Mr Wolf?	16